READING POWER

Technology That Changed the World

The Telescope
Looking into Space

Joanne Mattern

The Rosen Publishing Group's
PowerKids Press™
New York

Published in 2003 by The Rosen Publishing Group, Inc.
29 East 21st Street, New York, NY 10010

First Edition

Book Design: Michael DeLisio

Photo Credits: Cover, pp. 14, 19 © Roger Ressmeyer/Corbis; pp. 5, 6, 7, 9, 11, 13 © Bettman/Corbis; p. 8 © Gustavo Tomsich/Corbis; pp. 10, 12, (diagrams) Sam Jordan; p. 15 Courtesy of Nasa/JPL/Caltech; pp. 16–17 © Corbis; p. 18 Nasa/STSci; p. 21 Nasa, The Hubble Heritage Team

Library of Congress Cataloging-in-Publication Data

Mattern, Joanne, 1963-
The telescope: looking into space / Joanne Mattern.
    p. cm. — (Technology that changed the world)
Summary: An introduction to the telescope, including the history of its invention, how telescopes work, and information on different types of telescopes today.
Includes bibliographical references and index.
ISBN 0-8239-6489-2
1. Telescopes—Juvenile literature. [1. Telescopes.] I. Title.
QB88 .M3797 2003
681'.4123—dc21
                                    2002000528
]

Contents

Looking at the Sky

For thousands of years people have wondered what is in space. However, people of long ago had no way of looking closely at the sky. Over time, scientists invented tools, such as the telescope, to look at the stars, the Sun, and the other planets.

People have wondered about the mysteries of space for thousands of years.

At first, people used simple glass lenses to look at the sky. In 1608, Hans Lippershey of the Netherlands made a telescope. He placed two lenses in a tube and found that he could look at faraway objects much better.

Hans Lippershey worked with many different lenses.

Now You Know

Glass was first made around 3,000 B.C.

Lippershey's invention became very popular. Soon, other people became interested in his work.

Hans Lippershey was an eyeglass maker.

Galileo and His Telescope

One of the people interested in Lippershey's work was Galileo Galilei, an Italian scientist. In 1609, Galileo built a more powerful telescope. He discovered four of Jupiter's moons using his new telescope.

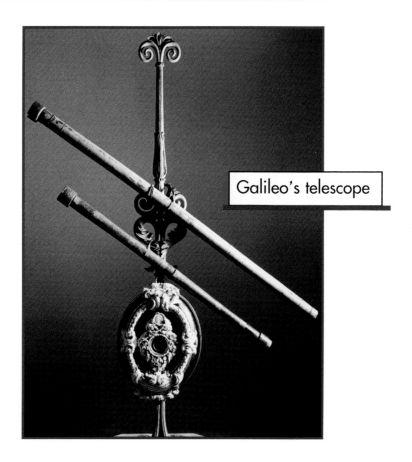

Galileo's telescope

Using his telescope, Galileo discovered that there were mountains on the Moon.

Galileo's telescope was a refracting telescope. His telescope used a lens to bend light to make objects look bigger. However, refracting telescopes sometimes made the images look fuzzy. Large refracting telescopes could not be made because the lenses they needed would be too heavy.

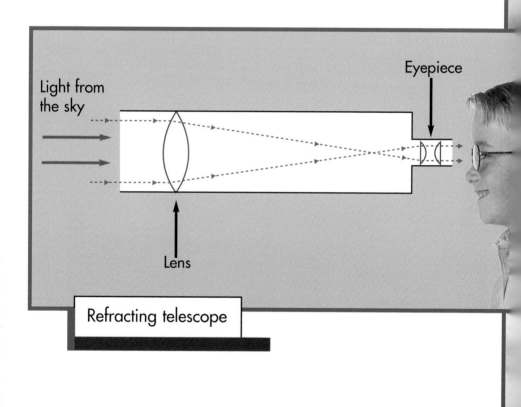

Light from the sky

Eyepiece

Lens

Refracting telescope

This painting shows Galileo telling someone how to use his refracting telescope.

Bigger and Better Telescopes

In 1611, Johannes Kepler, a German inventor, came up with an idea to improve the refracting telescope. In 1668, Isaac Newton, an English scientist, used Kepler's idea to build the first reflecting telescope. Newton's reflecting telescope used a curved mirror instead of a lens. The curved mirror bounced light to the viewer's eye to make an object look bigger.

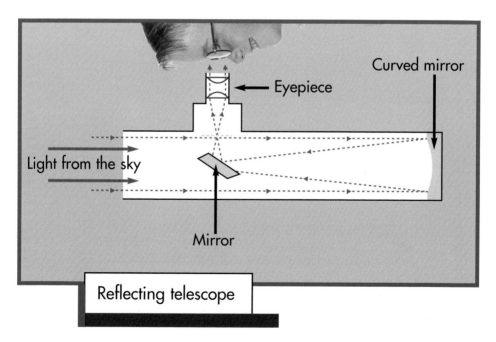

Reflecting telescope

Johannes Kepler was one of the first people to understand how the human eye uses light to see.

Isaac Newton studied different ways of using light.

Telescopes became so big they were placed in special buildings called observatories. Around 1825, the Dorpat Observatory was built in Estonia, a country near Russia. Its refracting telescope was 14 feet long and had a 9½-inch lens.

In 1949, a 200-inch reflecting telescope was built at Mount Palomar in California.

The dome of Mount Palomar's observatory can turn around in a complete circle. Big telescopes, like the one used at Mount Palomar, get clear images of objects in space.

The Keck Observatory in Hawaii has the largest telescope system on Earth. It has two 400-inch telescopes. It was built in 1996.

Space Telescopes

Scientists wanted to get even better images of objects in space. After years of tests, a satellite carrying a telescope was sent into space in 1983. The telescope was run mostly by computers.

This picture was made from information gathered by the satellite telescope in 1983.

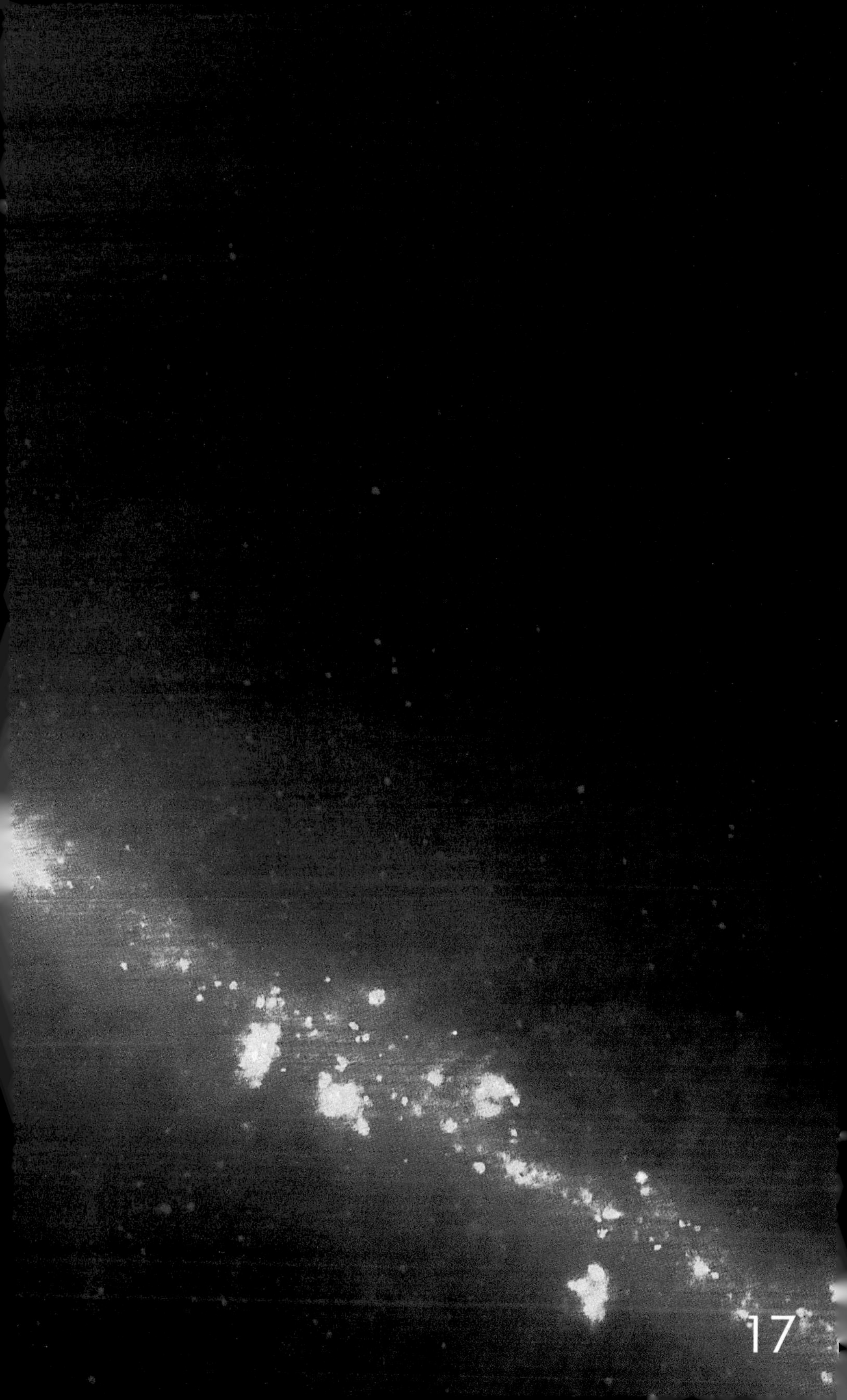

In 1990, the Hubble Space Telescope was flown into space aboard the space shuttle *Discovery*. Scientists are still using it today. The Hubble flies 380 miles above Earth and orbits the planet once about every 97 minutes. The Hubble sends clear pictures of faraway stars back to Earth.

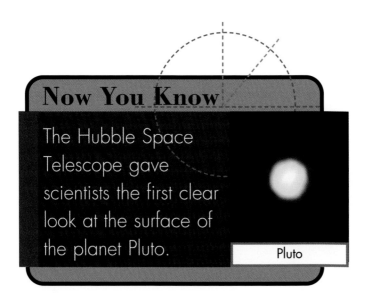

Now You Know

The Hubble Space Telescope gave scientists the first clear look at the surface of the planet Pluto.

Pluto

The Hubble Space Telescope is in position to be fixed by astronauts on the space shuttle Endeavour.

Telescopes of the Future

Today, scientists are making bigger and more powerful telescopes. They are working on a new telescope that will be put into orbit around the Sun — one million miles from Earth! This telescope will be able to see farther into space than even the Hubble telescope.

Telescopes have become the most important technology for unlocking the mysteries of space.

Time Line

1608: Hans Lippershey makes the first widely-used telescope.

1609: Galileo's refracting telescope becomes known throughout Europe.

1611: Johannes Kepler improves Galileo's telescope.

1668: Isaac Newton builds the first reflecting telescope.

1800s: Large observatories are built.

1949: A 200-inch telescope is built at Mount Palomar in California.

1983: A telescope is sent into space on a satellite.

1990: The Hubble Space Telescope is put into space.

1996: Two 400-inch telescopes are combined at the Keck Observatory in Hawaii to create the largest Earth telescope system.

This photo, taken by the Hubble Space Telescope, shows new stars being formed.

Glossary

future (**fyoo**-chuhr) a time that is to come

images (**ihm**-ihj-uhz) the likeness of objects or people made by a mirror or through a lens

lens (**lehnz**) a piece of curved glass that bends light rays

observatory (uhb-**zer**-vuh-tor-ee) a building that has telescopes and other tools for studying the stars, planets, and weather conditions

orbits (**or**-bihts) to travel around a planet or other body in space

reflecting (rih-**flehkt**-ihng) giving back or showing an image

refracting (rih-**frackt**-ihng) changing the image of an object by bending the light around it

satellite (**sat**-l-yt) a spacecraft that orbits Earth or another body in space

scientist (**sy**-uhn-tihst) a person who studies the world by using tests and experiments

surface (**ser**-fihs) the outside of anything

technology (tehk-**nahl**-uh-jee) to use knowledge and science to create an easier way of doing something

telescope (**tehl**-uh-skohp) a tool used to view faraway objects

Resources

Books

DK Space Encyclopedia
by Heather Couper and Nigel Henbest
DK Publishing (1999)

The Universe
by John Farndon
Millbrook Press (2001)

Web Sites

Due to the changing nature of Internet links, PowerKids
Press has developed an on-line list of Web sites related
to the subjects of this book. This site is updated regularly.
Please use this link to access the list:

http://www.powerkidslinks.com/tcw/tele/

Index

Word Count: 446

Note to Librarians, Teachers, and Parents
   If reading is a challenge, Reading Power is a solution! Reading Power is perfect for readers who want high-interest subject matter at an accessible reading level. These fact-filled, photo-illustrated books are designed for readers who want straightforward vocabulary, engaging topics, and a manageable reading experience. With clear picture/text correspondence, leveled Reading Power books put the reader in charge. Now readers have the power to get the information they want and the skills they need in a user-friendly format.